Lessons on Demand Presents

Study Guide Student Workbook for Where the Red Fern Grows

By:

John Pennington

The lessons on demand series is designed to provide ready to use resources for novel study. In this book you will find key vocabulary, student organizer pages, and assessments. This guide is the Student Workbook. The Teachers Guide will have answers and an open layout of the activities. The Student Workbook can be used alone but it will not include answers.

Look for bound print <u>Teacher Editions</u> on Amazon.com

PDF versions can be found on Teacherspayteachers.com

NAME:

TEACHER:

Date:

Vocabulary Box

Definition:

Draw:

Dormant

Related words:

Use in a sentence:

Definition:

Draw:

Devotion

Related words:

Use in a sentence:

NAME:

TEACHER:

Date:

Vocabulary Box

Definition:

Draw:

Grieve

Related words:

Use in a sentence:

Definition:

Draw:

Muzzle

Related words:

Use in a sentence:

NAME:

TEACHER:

Date:

Vocabulary Box

Definition:

Draw:

Fortune

Related words:

Use in a sentence:

Definition:

Draw:

Amends

Related words:

Use in a sentence:

NAME:

TEACHER:

Date:

Vocabulary Box

Definition:

Draw:

Sorghum

Related words:

Use in a sentence:

Definition:

Draw:

Muster

Related words:

Use in a sentence:

NAME:

TEACHER:

Date:

Vocabulary Box

Definition:

Draw:

Courage

Related words:

Use in a sentence:

Definition:

Draw:

Aggressive

Related words:

Use in a sentence:

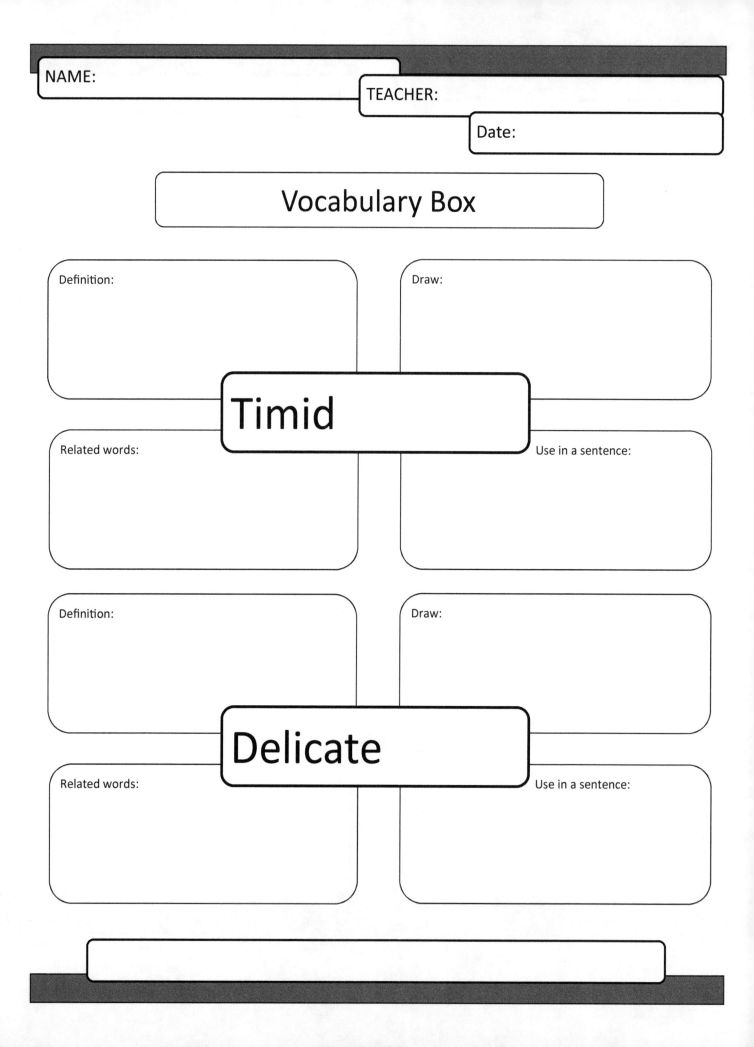

NAME:

TEACHER:

Date:

Test

Question: In what part of the United States does Billy live?

Answer:

Question: Where does Billy get his Dogs from?

Answer:

Question: Who gives Billy a pop and protects him when he gets in a fight?

Answer:

Question: What does Billy and his dogs hide from while in the cave?

Answer:

NAME:

TEACHER:

Date:

Assignment: Detail all of the jobs Billy does to raise money for his dogs. Use text support.

NAME: TEACHER: Date:

Character Sketch

Billy

Personality / Distinguishing marks

Connections to other characters

Draw a picture

Important Actions

NAME:

TEACHER:

Date:

Character Sketch

Papa

Personality/ Distinguishing marks

Draw a picture

Connections to other characters

Important Actions

NAME:

TEACHER:

Date:

Character Sketch

Mama

Personality/ Distinguishing marks

Connections to other characters

Draw a picture

Important Actions

NAME:

TEACHER:

Date:

Research connections

What am I researching? Ozarks

Source (URL, Book, Magazine, Interview)

Facts I found that could be useful or notes

1.

2.

3.

4.

5.

6.

NAME:

TEACHER:

Date:

Comic Strip

NAME:

TEACHER:

Date:

Lost Scene: Write a scene that takes place between _____ and _____

NAME:

TEACHER:

Date:

What would you do?

Character: _____

What did they do?

Example from text:

What would you do?

Why would that be better?

Character: _____

What did they do?

Example from text:

What would you do?

Why would that be better?

Character: _____

What did they do?

Example from text:

What would you do?

Why would that be better?

NAME:

TEACHER:

Date:

Assignment: <u>Discussion Questions</u>

Why do you think the first chapter tells the reader to expect from the rest of the book?

What have you wanted and how did you work to get it?

Compare and Contrast society then and society now.

NAME: TEACHER: Date:

Vocabulary Box

Definition:

Draw:

Obstacle

Related words:

Use in a sentence:

Definition:

Draw:

Peculiarity

Related words:

Use in a sentence:

NAME:

TEACHER:

Date:

Vocabulary Box

Definition:

Draw:

Persistence

Related words:

Use in a sentence:

Definition:

Draw:

Lantern

Related words:

Use in a sentence:

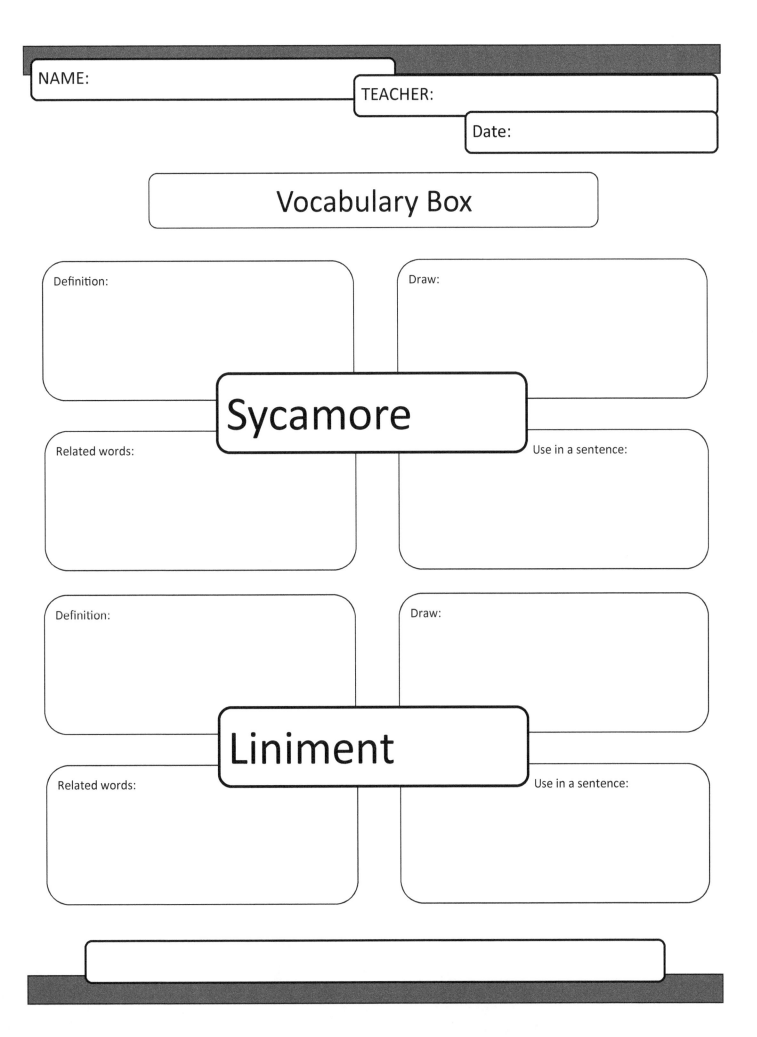

NAME:

TEACHER:

Date:

Vocabulary Box

Definition:

Draw:

Sympathy

Related words:

Use in a sentence:

Definition:

Draw:

Belligerent

Related words:

Use in a sentence:

NAME:
TEACHER:
Date:

Vocabulary Box

Definition:

Draw:

Slough

Related words:

Use in a sentence:

Definition:

Draw:

Trough

Related words:

Use in a sentence:

NAME:

TEACHER:

Date:

Vocabulary Box

Definition:

Draw:

Begrudgingly

Related words:

Use in a sentence:

Definition:

Draw:

Foliage

Related words:

Use in a sentence:

NAME:

TEACHER:

Date:

Test

Question: What was Billy's difficulty in getting his first coon?

Answer:

Question: What "miracle" happened to knock down the tree?

Answer:

Question: What item allowed Billy to save Little Ann from the freezing water?

Answer:

Question: Who died during the hunt for the Ghost Coon?

Answer:

NAME:

TEACHER:

Date:

Assignment: Establish a list of ways coons would try and trick the dogs. Use text support.

NAME:

TEACHER:

Date:

Character Sketch

Old Dan

Personality/ Distinguishing marks

Draw a picture

Connections to other characters

Important Actions

NAME:

TEACHER:

Date:

Character Sketch

Little Ann

Personality/ Distinguishing marks

Draw a picture

Connections to other characters

Important Actions

NAME:

TEACHER:

Date:

Character Sketch

Rubin Pritchard

Personality/ Distinguishing marks

Draw a picture

Connections to other characters

Important Actions

NAME:

TEACHER:

Date:

Character Sketch

Rainie Pritchard

Draw a picture

Personality/ Distinguishing marks

Connections to other characters

Important Actions

NAME:

TEACHER:

Date:

Draw the Scene: What five things have you included in the scene?

1	2	3

4	5

NAME:

TEACHER:

Date:

Precognition Sheet

Who ?

What's going to happen?

What will be the result?

Who ?

What's going to happen?

What will be the result?

Who ?

What's going to happen?

What will be the result?

Who ?

What's going to happen?

What will be the result?

How many did you get correct?

NAME:

TEACHER:

Date:

Sequencing or timeline

1.

2.

3.

4.

5.

NAME:

TEACHER:

Date:

Who, What, When, Where, and How

Who

What

Where

When

How

NAME:

TEACHER:

Date:

Assignment: <u>Discussion Questions</u>

Why is hunting so important to Billy?

Why does Grand Paw put a bar of soap in Billy's back pocket?

Are the Pritchard boys evil?

NAME:

TEACHER:

Date:

Vocabulary Box

Definition:

Draw:

Solemn

Related words:

Use in a sentence:

Definition:

Draw:

Dumbfounded

Related words:

Use in a sentence:

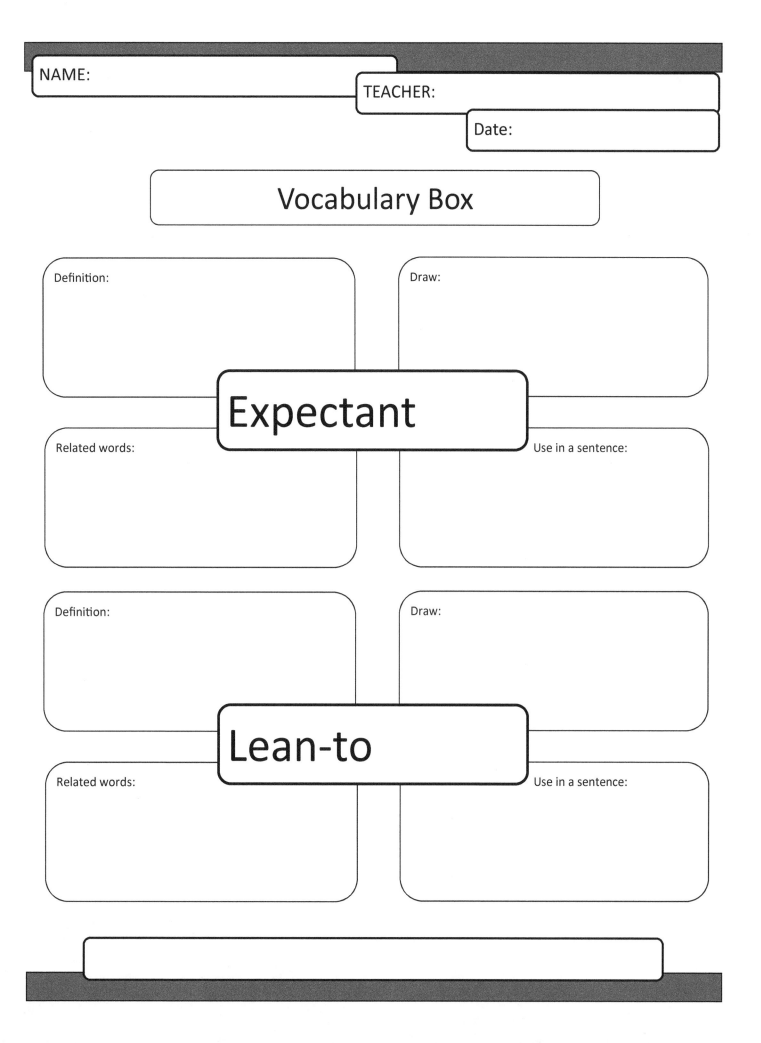

NAME:

TEACHER:

Date:

Vocabulary Box

Definition:

Draw:

Monotonous

Related words:

Use in a sentence:

Definition:

Draw:

Eerie

Related words:

Use in a sentence:

NAME:

TEACHER:

Date:

Vocabulary Box

Definition:

Draw:

Superstition

Related words:

Use in a sentence:

Definition:

Draw:

Jinx

Related words:

Use in a sentence:

NAME:

TEACHER:

Date:

Vocabulary Box

Definition:

Draw:

Rhythmic

Related words:

Use in a sentence:

Definition:

Draw:

Blizzard

Related words:

Use in a sentence:

NAME:

TEACHER:

Date:

Vocabulary Box

Definition:

Draw:

Predatory

Related words:

Use in a sentence:

Definition:

Draw:

Lithe

Related words:

Use in a sentence:

NAME:

TEACHER:

Date:

Create the Test

Question: What is Billy given at camp that makes him feel like he is finally a man?

Answer:

Question: Who is hurt and needs medical care during the championship hunt?

Answer:

Question: What is responsible for killing Old Dan?

Answer:

Question: What plant grows between Old Dan and Little Ann?

Answer:

NAME:

TEACHER:

Date:

Assignment: Designate all the actions in the story that could be divine intervention.

NAME:

TEACHER:

Date:

Character Sketch

Grand Paw

Draw a picture

Personality/ Distinguishing marks

Connections to other characters

Important Actions

NAME:

TEACHER:

Date:

Create the Test

Question:

Answer:

Question:

Answer:

Question:

Answer:

Question:

Answer:

NAME:

TEACHER:

Date:

Draw the Scene: What five things have you included in the scene?

1   2   3
4   5

NAME:

TEACHER:

Date:

Assignment: Pyramid

NAME:

TEACHER:

Date:

Who, What, When, Where, and How

Who

What

Where

When

How

NAME:

TEACHER:

Date:

Assignment: <u>Discussion Questions</u>

How do you feel about Little Ann and the beauty contest?

What do you think was the cause of Little Ann's death?

How does the events of the story effect Billy's future?

How does the first chapter change in meaning after completing the story?

NAME:

TEACHER:

Date:

Advertisement: Draw an advertisement for _____

NAME:

TEACHER:

Date:

Chapter to Poem

Assignment: Select 20 words found in the chapter to create a poem where each line is 3 words long.

Title:

NAME:

TEACHER:

Date:

Character Sketch

Name

Personality/ Distinguishing marks

Draw a picture

Connections to other characters

Important Actions

NAME:

TEACHER:

Date:

Comic Strip

NAME:

TEACHER:

Date:

Compare and Contrast Venn Diagram

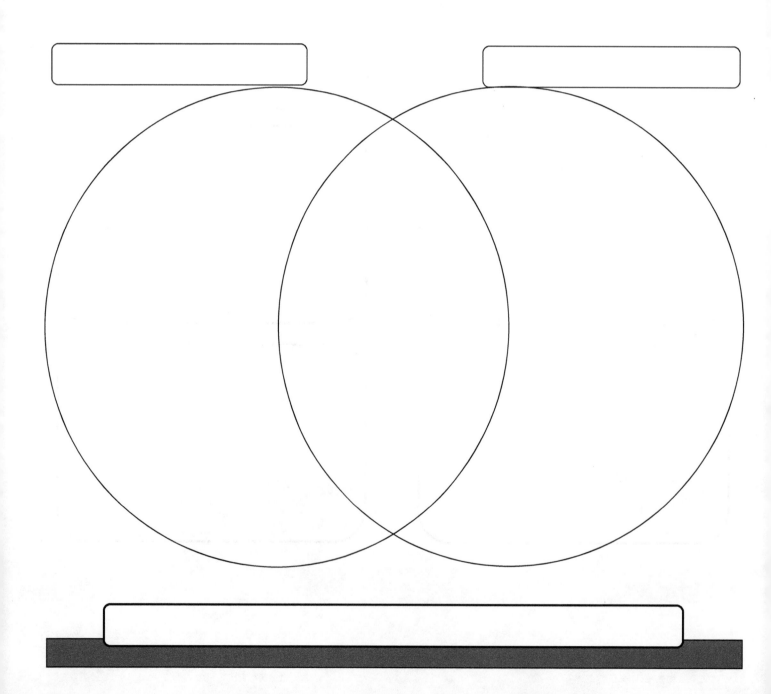

NAME:

TEACHER:

Date:

Create the Test

Question:

Answer:

Question:

Answer:

Question:

Answer:

Question:

Answer:

NAME:

TEACHER:

Date:

Draw the Scene: What five things have you included in the scene?

1   2   3

4   5

NAME:

TEACHER:

Date:

Interview: Who _____

Question:

Answer:

Question:

Answer:

Question:

Answer:

Question:

Answer:

NAME:

TEACHER:

Date:

Lost Scene: Write a scene that takes place between _____ and _____

NAME:

TEACHER:

Date:

Making Connections

What is the connection?

NAME:

TEACHER:

Date:

Precognition Sheet

Who ?

What's going to happen?

What will be the result?

Who ?

What's going to happen?

What will be the result?

Who ?

What's going to happen?

What will be the result?

Who ?

What's going to happen?

What will be the result?

How many did you get correct?

NAME:

TEACHER:

Date:

Assignment: Pyramid

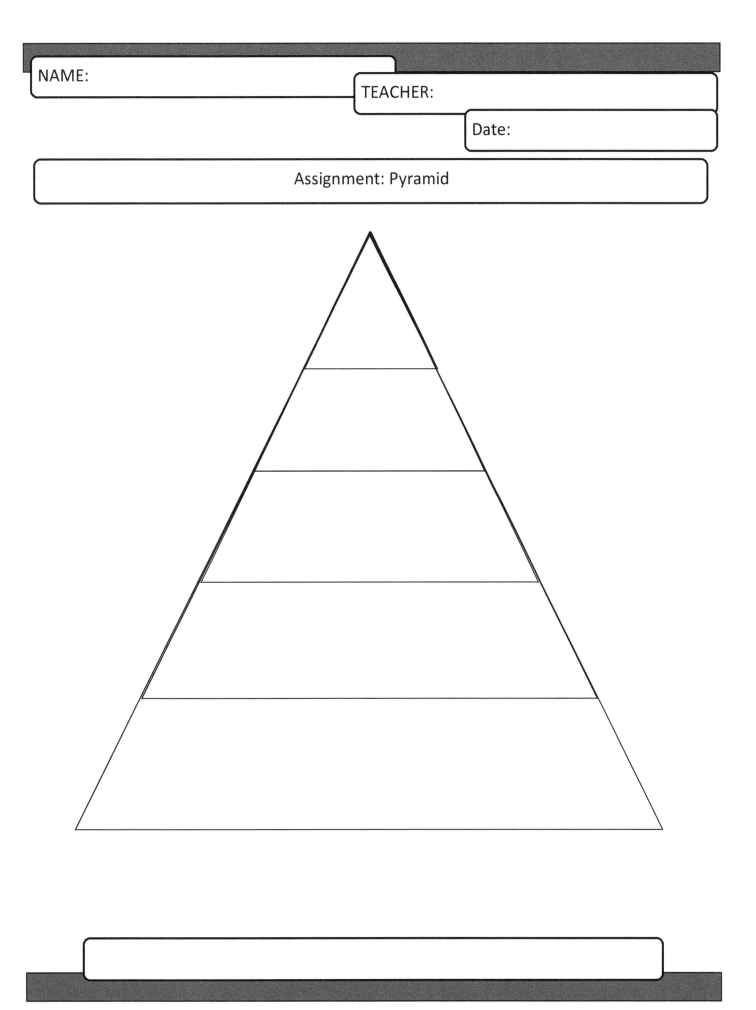

NAME:

TEACHER:

Date:

Research connections

What am I researching?

Source (URL, Book, Magazine, Interview)

Facts I found that could be useful or notes

1.

2.

3.

4.

5.

6.

NAME:

TEACHER:

Date:

Sequencing or timeline

1.

2.

3.

4.

5.

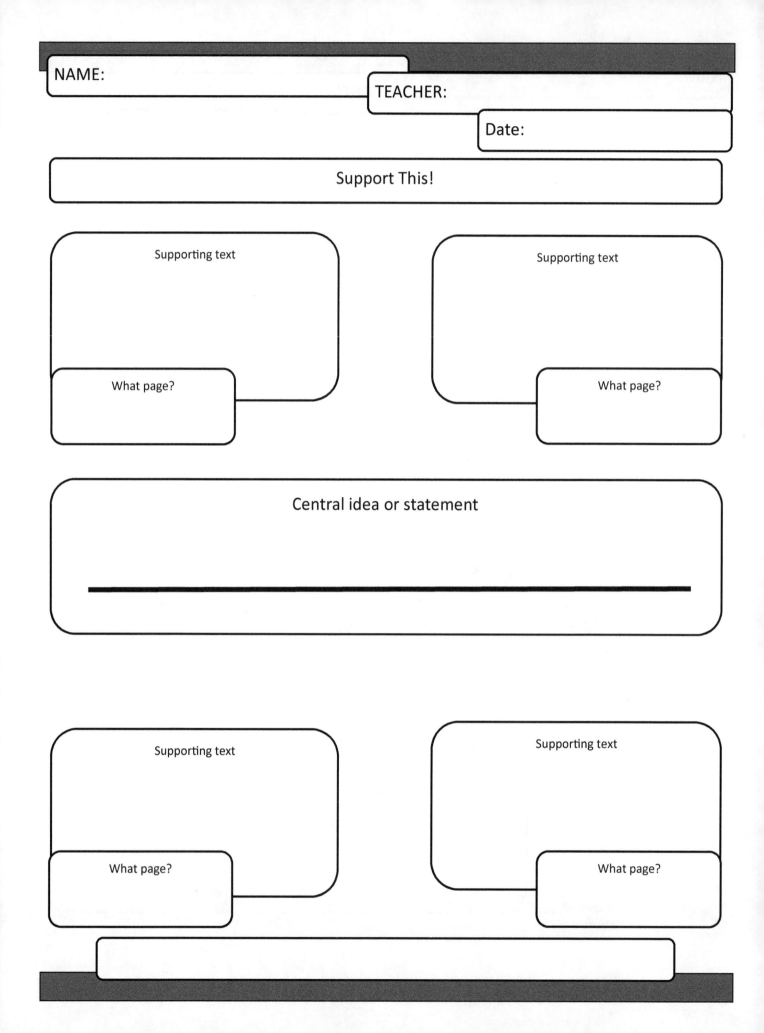

NAME:

TEACHER:

Date:

Travel Brochure

Why should you visit?

What are you going to see?

Map

Special Events

NAME:

TEACHER:

Date:

Top Ten List

1.

2.

3.

4.

5.

6.

7.

8.

9.

10.

NAME:

TEACHER:

Date:

Vocabulary Box

Definition:

Draw:

Word:

Related words:

Use in a sentence:

Definition:

Draw:

Word:

Related words:

Use in a sentence:

NAME:

TEACHER:

Date:

What would you do?

Character: _____

What did they do?

Example from text:

What would you do?

Why would that be better?

Character: _____

What did they do?

Example from text:

What would you do?

Why would that be better?

Character: _____

What did they do?

Example from text:

What would you do?

Why would that be better?

NAME:

TEACHER:

Date:

Who, What, When, Where, and How

Who

What

Where

When

How

NAME:

TEACHER:

Date:

Write a letter

To:

From:

NAME:

TEACHER:

Date:

Assignment:

NAME:

TEACHER:

Date:

Add a Character

Who is the new character?

What reason does the new character have for being there?

Write a dialog between the new character and characters currently in the scene.

You dialog must be 6 lines or more, and can occur in the beginning, middle or end of the scene.

NAME:

TEACHER:

Date:

Costume Design

Draw a costume for one the characters in the scene.

Why do you believe this character should have a costume like this?

NAME:

TEACHER:

Date:

Props Needed

Prop:

What text from the scene supports this?

Prop:

What text from the scene supports this?

Prop:

What text from the scene supports this?

NAME:

TEACHER:

Date:

Soundtrack!

Song:

Why should this song be used?

Song:

Why should this song be used?

Song:

Why should this song be used?

NAME:

TEACHER:

Date:

Stage Directions

List who is moving, how they are moving and use text from the dialog to determine when they move.

Who:

How:

When:

Who:

How:

When:

Who:

How:

When:

NAME:

TEACHER:

Date:

Poetry Analysis

Name of Poem:

Subject:
- Text Support:

Plot:
- Text Support:

Theme:
- Text Support:

Setting:
- Text Support:

Tone:
- Text Support:

Important Words and Phrases:

Why are these words and phrases important:

CPSIA information can be obtained
at www.ICGtesting.com
Printed in the USA
LVHW060955130123
737109LV00014B/172